TROMBONE

2ND EDITION

To access audio visit:
www.halleonard.com/mylibrary

Enter Code
1527-8933-3118-6341

Audio Arrangements by Peter Deneff

ISBN 978-1-6780-577-6

HAL•LEONARD®
CORPORATION
7777 W. BLUEMOUND RD. P.O. BOX 13819 MILWAUKEE, WI 53213

Visit Hal Leonard Online at
www.halleonard.com

BACK TO DECEMBER

Words and Music by
TAYLOR SWIFT

TROMBONE

BLANK SPACE

TROMBONE

Words and Music by TAYLOR SWIFT,
MAX MARTIN and SHELLBACK

FIFTEEN

TROMBONE

Words and Music by
TAYLOR SWIFT

I KNEW YOU WERE TROUBLE

TROMBONE

Words and Music by TAYLOR SWIFT,
SHELLBACK and MAX MARTIN

LOVE STORY

TROMBONE

Words and Music by
TAYLOR SWIFT

MEAN

TROMBONE

Words and Music by
TAYLOR SWIFT

OUR SONG

TROMBONE

Words and Music by
TAYLOR SWIFT

PICTURE TO BURN

TROMBONE

Words and Music by TAYLOR SWIFT
and LIZ ROSE

SHAKE IT OFF

TROMBONE

Words and Music by TAYLOR SWIFT,
MAX MARTIN and SHELLBACK

20

SHOULD'VE SAID NO

TROMBONE

Words and Music by
TAYLOR SWIFT

TEARDROPS ON MY GUITAR

TROMBONE

Words and Music by TAYLOR SWIFT
and LIZ ROSE

22

TROMBONE

Words and Music by TAYLOR SWIFT,
SHELLBACK and MAX MARTIN

25

WE ARE NEVER EVER GETTING BACK TOGETHER

TROMBONE

Words and Music by TAYLOR SWIFT,
SHELLBACK and MAX MARTIN

WHITE HORSE

TROMBONE

Words and Music by TAYLOR SWIFT
and LIZ ROSE

YOU BELONG WITH ME

TROMBONE

Words and Music by TAYLOR SWIFT
and LIZ ROSE